V is for von Trapp

A Musical Family Alphabet

Story of the legendary family who inspired *The Sound of Music*

Written by William Anderson
Illustrated by Linda Dockey Graves

To my own family members,
who have enjoyed so many visits to the Trapp Family Lodge.

—Bill

To the memory of my mother and father, Priscilla and Merritt,
who were true Vermonters.

—Linda

Sleeping Bear Press™

2395 South Huron Parkway, Suite 200, Ann Arbor, MI 48104
www.sleepingbearpress.com

Printed and bound in the United States.

10 9 8 7 6 5 4

Library of Congress Cataloging-in-Publication Data

Anderson, William, V is for von Trapp : a musical family alphabet / written by William Anderson ;
illustrated by Linda Graves.
p. cm.
ISBN 978-1-58536-531-9
1. Trapp Family Singers--Juvenile literature. 2. Alphabet books.
I. Graves, Linda Dockey, ill. II. Title.
ML3930.T7A53 2010
782.5092'2--dc22
[B]
2010010741

Oftentimes, the best stories are really true. The movie called *The Sound of Music* is one of them.

The Sound of Music is based on the life of Austria's von Trapp family. Many of the events in the film truly happened, including the arrival of Maria Kutschera at Captain Georg von Trapp's home to teach one of his seven motherless children. Later, Maria became the widowed Captain's wife and a second mother to his children.

The von Trapps lived through difficult and dangerous times in the world's history. In the 1930s Germany's powerful Nazi Party threatened the world's peace. In 1938 the Nazis seized Austria. The von Trapps escaped the Nazis' grip and came to America. Here they found freedom. Like millions of immigrants before them, they were welcomed to a new homeland, America.

The von Trapps made America their permanent home. As a singing, performing family, they enriched our diverse culture.

THE · VON · TRAPP · FAMILY · TREE

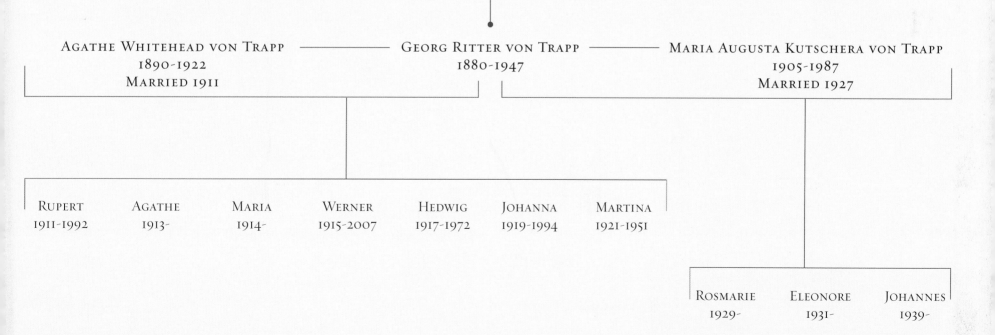

AGATHE WHITEHEAD VON TRAPP
1890-1922
MARRIED 1911

GEORG RITTER VON TRAPP
1880-1947

MARIA AUGUSTA KUTSCHERA VON TRAPP
1905-1987
MARRIED 1927

RUPERT
1911-1992

AGATHE
1913-

MARIA
1914-

WERNER
1915-2007

HEDWIG
1917-1972

JOHANNA
1919-1994

MARTINA
1921-1951

ROSMARIE
1929-

ELEONORE
1931-

JOHANNES
1939-

When we think of Austria, we think of mountains and music.

The Alps mountains cover nearly 75 percent of Austria. On the lower slopes, trees grow; higher up, there are mountain meadows. Even higher there are regions of rock, ice, and glaciers. In the valleys, villages, and farms, Austrians share their family traditions with each new generation.

High in the Alps grows the white star-shaped flower called edelweiss. It is hard to find, and dangerous to reach in hidden crevices. At one time young men sought the white flower for their sweethearts. Bringing the rare blossoms proved their love—and bravery.

It is often said that music is Austria's gift to the world. The Christmas carol "Silent Night" was first heard there in 1818. Austrian composers Joseph Haydn, Franz Schubert, and Johann Strauss created symphonies, operas, church music, and waltzes. Wolfgang Amadeus Mozart, born in Salzburg in 1756, was Austria's most popular composer.

Salzburg was the home of the von Trapp family. In the 1930s they began performing as a singing family. Their early life, told in *The Sound of Music*, introduced millions to Austria's mighty snow-covered mountains, and its love of music.

A is for Austria
 where mountains touch the sky,
  and peaks are capped by snow and ice.
Look close! There's edelweiss!

Georg von Trapp sailed the seas of the world as a navy cadet. Back home in Austria he attended a ball, where he spied a beautiful young lady playing the violin. She was Agathe Whitehead. After a two-year courtship, Georg and Agathe were married in 1911.

Their first two children were Rupert and Agathe. During World War I (1914–1918) Captain von Trapp served Austria's navy as a submarine commander. The Captain served his country well. He was awarded Austria's highest honor, the Maria Theresian medal.

While the Captain was away at war, his family lived at their grandmother Whitehead's lakeside home near Zell-am-See. There Maria, Werner, and Hedwig were born. Papa made short visits from his duties. What joy when he came home and played his violin and guitar. Mama joined in on piano. "There was so much music going on in homes like ours," said Rupert. (In Austrian families, like the von Trapps, Pa*pa* and Ma*ma* were pronounced with emphasis on the second syllable.)

In 1918 the war ended. Papa returned home. With so many children, Papa created a code for each, using his Navy whistle. When the whistle trilled their name codes, the children rushed to Papa. They never marched, but they were his little sailors.

B is for Brothers and sisters—
seven siblings in all.
Each of them came running
when they heard Papa's whistle call!

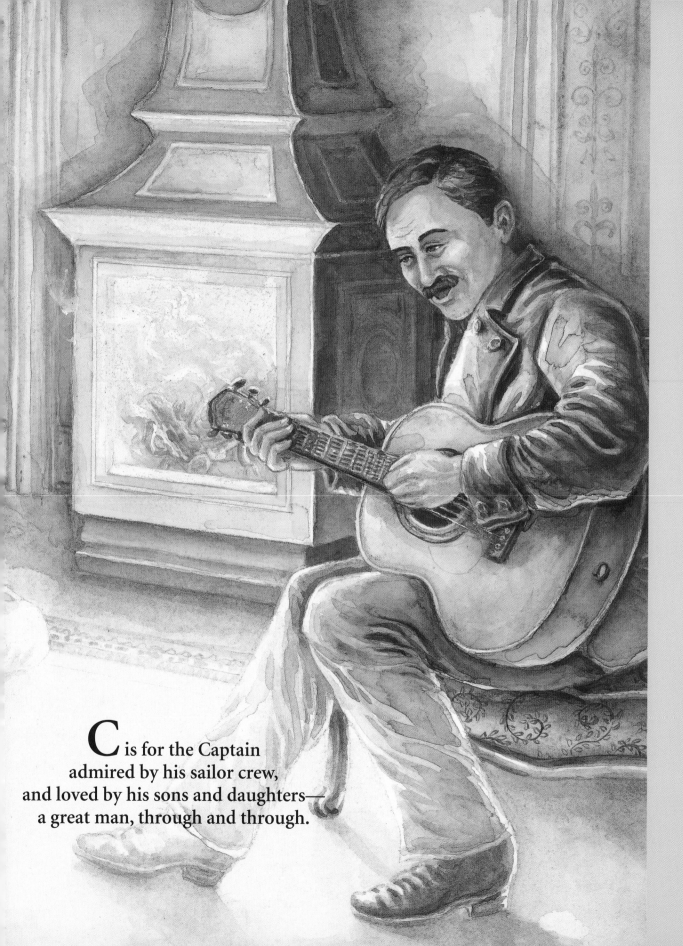

After the war Austria lost its navy. There were no more ships for the Captain to sail. He returned home to his family in Zell-am-See.

The Captain found a spacious home for the family in Vienna. It included a playroom and a schoolroom for the older children. After lessons Papa joined in games, told stories, and taught the children to play the guitar, violin, and accordion. "Music was around us all the time," daughter Maria said.

Mama was a kindly, loving mother. She kept her growing family happy and organized. They picnicked, skied, went to concerts, to church, and to the circus.

Then an epidemic of scarlet fever raged through Vienna. The children were very sick. Even worse, Mama also caught the disease. She could not recover, and in 1922 she died. The house became a quieter place—a home without a mother.

C is for the Captain
admired by his sailor crew,
and loved by his sons and daughters—
a great man, through and through.

In 1925 the Captain moved his children to a new home in Salzburg, a beautiful fortress city surrounded by mountains. Villa Trapp, their large, new home, was just outside town. Now the children attended school in Salzburg. But twelve-year-old Maria was not strong enough to walk so far. Papa found a tutor to teach her at home. Maria Augusta Kutschera, a student nun from Nonnberg Abbey, became the tutor. Another Maria!

Maria Kutschera was Nonnberg's tomboy, whistling hymns, sliding down banisters, and running instead of walking. She did not want to leave the abbey for Villa Trapp. But Maria learned from the nuns to follow God's plan for her life.

After giving young Maria her lessons, the new teacher befriended the other children. She played games, told stories, went hiking with them, and sang and strummed her guitar. And she wanted to sing with them! How beautifully their voices blended!

The Captain wanted a second mother for his children, someone who loved them. He asked Maria to marry him. But she couldn't be a wife, a mother, and a nun. Maria prayed for God's plan. The answer came; she agreed to marry the Captain.

D is for the Decision,
one that changed Maria's life,
becoming a second mother
and a navy captain's wife.

Dd

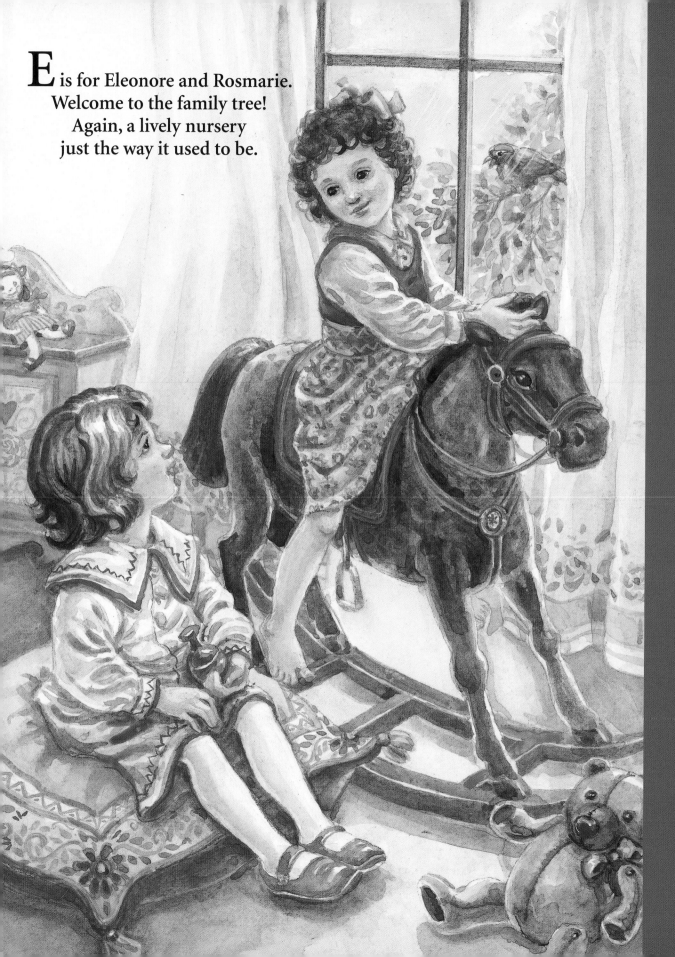

E is for Eleonore and Rosmarie.
Welcome to the family tree!
Again, a lively nursery
just the way it used to be.

The Captain and Maria Kutschera were married at the abbey in 1927. "The Captain was so kind, so understanding," Maria said. "I grew to love him very much." Maria was busy learning to keep the household running smoothly for the family. She read books about housekeeping and being a mother. To set Maria apart from the Captain's first wife, the children called her "Mother." Friends and relatives did the same, or used "Mother Trapp."

In 1929 Maria became a mother herself. Rosmarie, the sixth von Trapp daughter, was born. Two years later Eleonore arrived. The older children adored their pretty new sisters. Hedwig tended the little girls in their nursery. Papa told them exciting bedtime tales.

During vacations the family went camping and sailing. The Captain led them on adventures through the seas he'd traveled during his navy days. One summer they camped on an island and stayed until school started.

As the seven older children grew, they showed many talents: Rupert planned to be a doctor, while Agathe studied art and languages. Maria and Werner went to music school. Hedwig was clever at most everything. Johanna and Martina both were artistic.

Ee

"We sang for the joy of singing," said Maria von Trapp of the family's hobby. The combination of their voices—sopranos, altos, a tenor, and a bass—created a family choir. They sang *a cappella*, with no instruments, just their voices.

Austrian tradition was full of folk songs, and the von Trapps sang dozens of them. The family learned music from the sixteenth, seventeenth, and eighteenth centuries. They sang for services in the village church. "When you sing, you pray twice," Mother told them.

Villa Trapp had its own chapel. When Father Franz Wasner conducted services there, he heard the family sing. Father Wasner was a musician and choirmaster and soon he was coaching the singers. The house resounded with music!

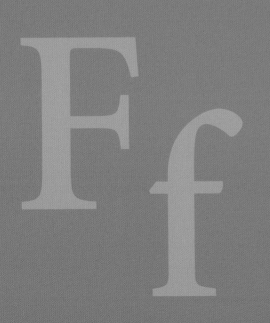

Ff

F is for Family of Singers.
Sopranos, altos, a tenor, a bass
joined in daily sing-alongs.
Villa Trapp was filled with songs!

Lotte Lehmann was a famous opera singer who often sang at the Salzburg Music Festival. One day in 1936 she arrived at Villa Trapp, asking to rent the house while she performed in town. She overheard Mother and the children singing. She was overwhelmed!

"Children, this is wonderful!" she exclaimed. "You must give concerts; you must go to America! You have voices of gold!"

"I thought she was joking," the Captain later said. "She told us we were great artists whom the world should hear."

Lotte Lehmann persuaded the family to enter a singing competition at the Salzburg Festival. They sang some folk songs, and to their surprise, they won! Then they sang on Austrian radio. The next invitation took them to Belvedere Palace in Vienna, to sing for government officials.

At first, Captain von Trapp was uncomfortable with his family singing in public. But he accepted their performing and supported them. As Werner said, "When we have talents, we must share them."

Gg

G is for "Voices of Gold."
"Sing in a contest!" they were told.
Back came the judges' replies:
the von Trapps win first prize.

Singing was the family hobby and so was hiking. Villa Trapp was at the foot of Gaisberg Mountain, and the family knew its trails to the top. For longer trips they packed knapsacks and took the train into the foothills of the towering Alps. Singing and climbing, everyone admired mountain lakes, farms, churches, and chalets along the way.

"Wherever there are mountains, people sing!" Mother said.

Then the family was invited to make their first concert tour. They sang in France, Italy, Belgium, Holland, and England. Father Wasner conducted each concert. He selected their music and arranged it. The concerts included folk songs, ballads, yodels, and early music composed for church services. Instrumental music was performed. Family members played recorders, which are flute-like instruments. Werner played the viola da gamba, a stringed instrument of the fifteenth century. Father Wasner played the spinet, an early form of the piano.

The von Trapps became as familiar with performing on stage as they were with hiking the mountain trails.

H is for Hiking,
with folk songs along the way.
Climbing mountains higher and higher,
a perfect holiday!

The Captain disliked the Nazi Party that ruled Germany. Its evil leader, Adolf Hitler, was eager for more territory, including nearby Austria. On March 12, 1938, it happened—Germany invaded Austria. Soldiers marched across the German border into Austria.

Church bells all over Salzburg rang. The Captain called the police, asking why. They said that the Nazis were being "welcomed." Those who were against the Nazis risked being imprisoned. The Captain was ordered to fly a Nazi flag on the house. He wouldn't. The family was asked to sing on the radio to honor Hitler's birthday. They refused. The Captain was summoned to serve the German Navy. He said no.

Saying no to the Nazis was risky. The von Trapps knew they no longer could stay in Austria. Papa said each family member must agree to leave; otherwise they would all stay. Everyone said yes. Secret plans were made to leave. Their destination was America. The family was fortunate; they had an invitation to sing concerts there.

Ii

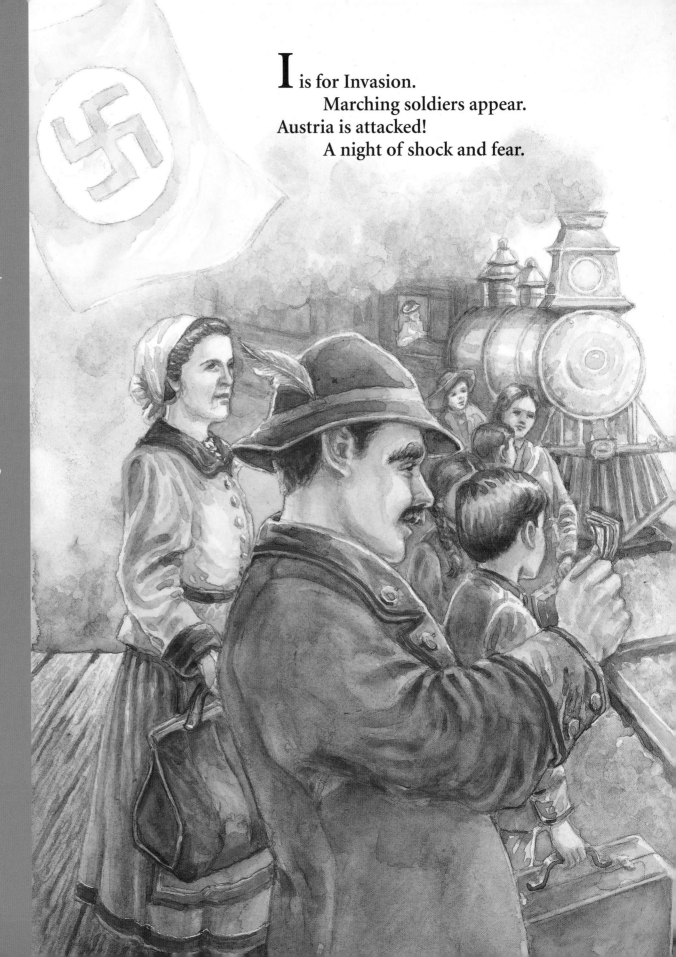

I is for Invasion.
Marching soldiers appear.
Austria is attacked!
A night of shock and fear.

On the day they left Austria, the von Trapps dressed as if they were leaving for a hike. At the railway station, they bought tickets and the train chugged away to Italy. They didn't know when they would see their house again. The von Trapps prayed for God's protection on their journey.

There were twelve in the escape group: Papa, Mother, the nine children, and Father Wasner. After a short stay in Italy, they went to England where they boarded a ship to America. The ship reached New York harbor after a long voyage across the Atlantic.

What skyscrapers the family saw in New York! So many new sights! A big blue bus arrived to take the Trapp Family Singers on their first American tour. Each night audiences applauded their singing. Each day they traveled to the next city.

"We have come over to bring the best of old Austria, its art, singing, and customs," the Captain said.

When the first concert tour ended, new friends found a house in Philadelphia for the family. Johannes, the tenth and last von Trapp child, was born there.

J j

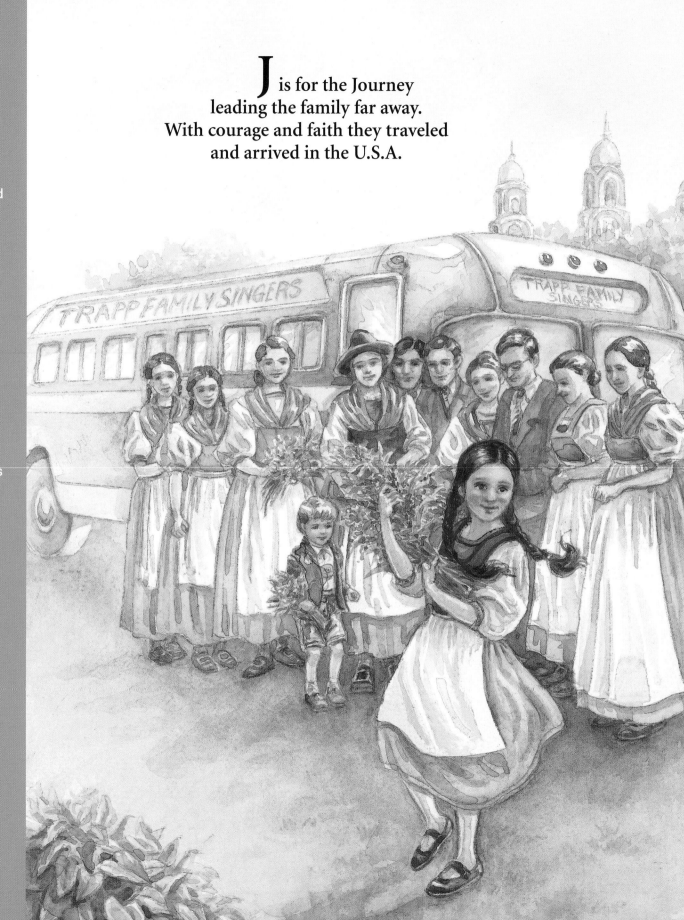

J is for the Journey
leading the family far away.
With courage and faith they traveled
and arrived in the U.S.A.

Kristkindl is our name for K.
He's the reason for each Christmas day.
A glowing tree, a festive sight,
and "Silent Night" sung by candlelight.

The family's concert tours started in the fall and ended in the spring. During December the Trapp Family Singers brought Austrian Christmas music to their audiences. Christmas is Austria's most important holiday, but Santa Claus is unknown there. On December 6, St. Nicholas learns good deeds—and bad ones—of children. He leaves treats for the well-behaved. On Christmas Eve, Kristkindl, the Christ Child, leaves gifts beneath the Christmas tree. "We brought our Christmas with us across the Atlantic Ocean," said Mother.

At holiday concerts, the von Trapps filed onstage with lanterns when the curtain opened. They sang Christmas music of many countries. Between the songs, Mother told of Christmas customs. The final song was "Silent Night." Mother's ancestors, the Rainer family singers, brought the carol to America in the 1840s. A century later, it created a memorable moment as the von Trapps sang it, then quietly left the stage. Audiences sat spellbound.

The Christmas concerts were unforgettable. "God used our concerts to touch hearts," said Eleonore. "Peace settled on the audience each time we sang."

K k

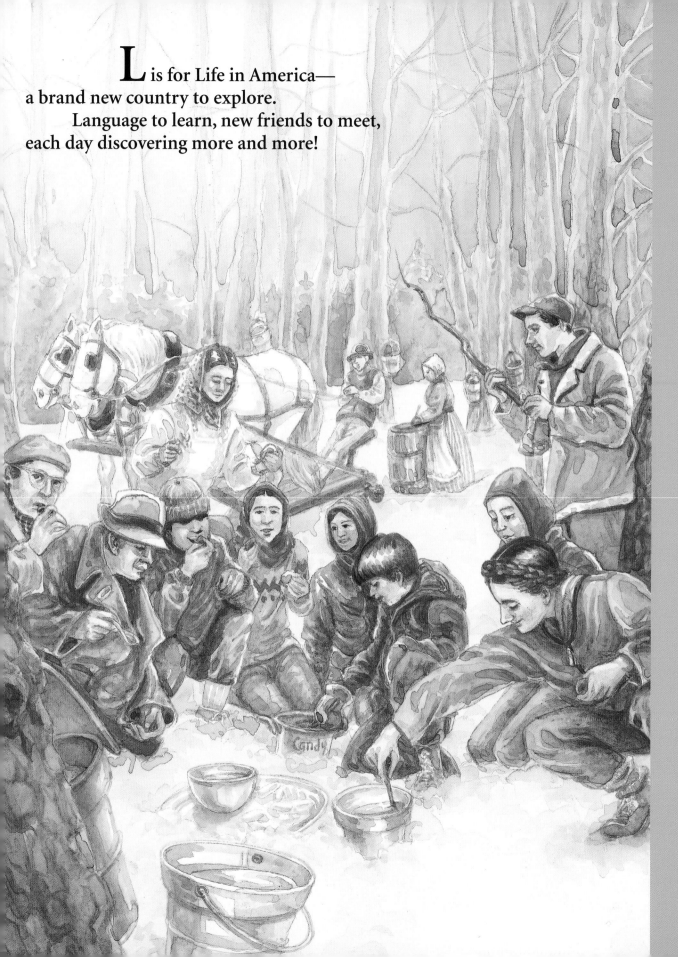

L is for Life in America—
a brand new country to explore.
    Language to learn, new friends to meet,
each day discovering more and more!

America welcomed the von Trapps. The family loved America's freedom and diversity. No one minded their Austrian accents and clothes. People were friendly. The public was interested in the von Trapps' music and their lives at home in Philadelphia.

On tour Mother arranged trips to museums and national parks, where the family learned about America. They visited historic places and even sang at The White House.

Everyone in the family learned English. American folk songs were added to the concerts. While the family traveled, Rosmarie and Eleonore attended boarding school. They learned English quickly. A crib was set up for Johannes in the bus. He was surrounded by singing.

America entered World War II in December, 1941. The news came to the von Trapps during a concert. Mother announced the war news to a shocked audience. Together the family and their audience sang "My Country 'tis of Thee."

Ll

Maria von Trapp's family credits her for helping to lead them from Austria to America. Her energy and leadership were as strong as a mountain. She persuaded a concert agent to manage the Trapp Family Singers. They became very popular, often singing more than 100 concerts each year.

During concerts Maria was the spokesperson. She explained the music, speaking very formally. Then, in Denver, a fly buzzed around the stage during a song. Maria took a breath; in flew the fly! She choked and coughed, embarrassed. No longer proper, she explained: "I swallowed a fly."

Everyone laughed. The concert was not ruined; instead Maria knew the concertgoers *wanted* her to relax. From then on, Maria told each audience: "You are guests at our musical party."

Maria's storytelling led her to write her first book, *The Story of the Trapp Family Singers*. The book was the basis of the musical play, *The Sound of Music*.

M m

M is for Maria von Trapp, mother, storyteller, and musician. With her strong determination she told of her family's tradition.

In 1942 the von Trapps vacationed in Stowe, Vermont, a village in the Green Mountains. Nearby was Mount Mansfield, Vermont's highest mountain. Once again the family hiked, and views everywhere reminded them of Austria. They chose Stowe for their permanent American home.

They found a farm overlooking mountain ranges and valleys. The view was gorgeous, but the house was small and in poor condition. Mother said: "We can build a house, but we can't build a view." They bought the farm. Part of the old house collapsed in a storm. The family rebuilt much of the house themselves. When it was done, it looked like an Austrian house with flower boxes on the balconies.

Between tours, the family worked on the farm. Everyone had special duties caring for the house, the farm animals, gardens, orchards, and fields. "We were like a pioneer family," said Rosmarie.

N is for the New Home,
a shabby farmhouse, yes, true.
But the family bought it, not for the house
but for the beautiful mountain view.

N n

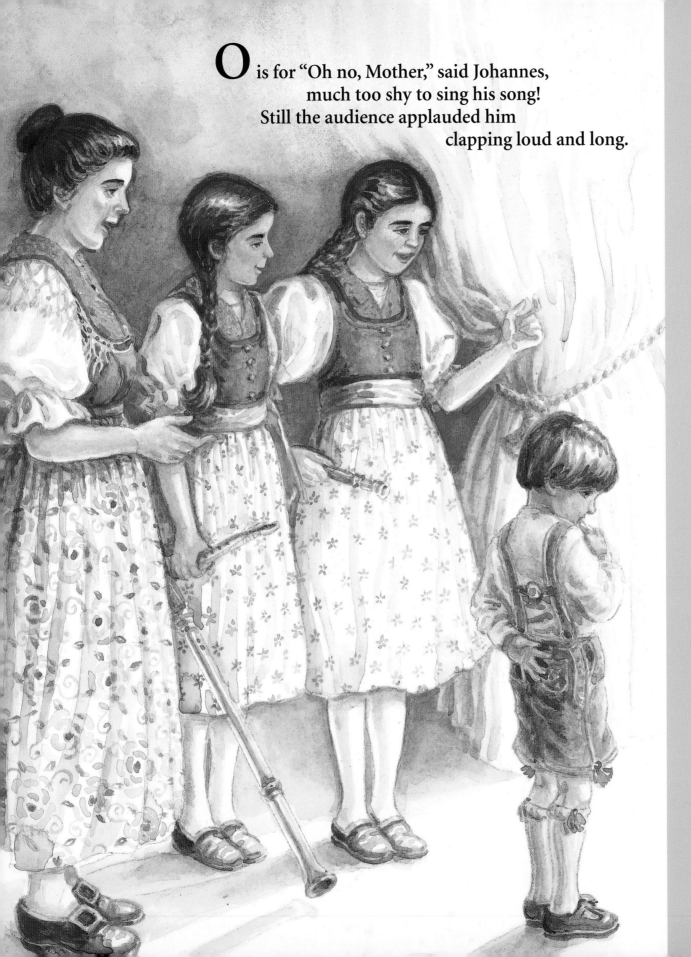

O is for "Oh no, Mother," said Johannes,
much too shy to sing his song!
Still the audience applauded him
clapping loud and long.

In 1943 Rupert and Werner joined the U.S. Army to fight the Nazis in Europe. The von Trapps were lonesome for their boys, just as many other American families were for theirs.

The Trapp Family Singers sang on. Rosmarie and Eleonore joined the group in place of their brothers. The girls did their school work while traveling. Father Wasner and other family members helped with the tutoring. The von Trapps were a homeschooling family.

When Johannes was four, he studied recorder with sister Maria. At a concert he asked to sing "Old MacDonald had a Farm." All alone, he sang the song. But the loud clapping after the song scared him. At the next concert Mother asked him to sing. "No!" he said firmly. Even without a song, the audience applauded him again! Johannes lived on a farm, but he did not want to sing about a farm!

Oo

Many Americans wanted their families to sing like the Trapp Family Singers. Mother had an idea: why not open a music camp, and show them how?

At the edge of the von Trapp farm stood an abandoned camp. The state of Vermont gave Mother permission to use it. The von Trapps worked to make the camp comfortable for guests.

Buildings were named for composers: Bach, Beethoven, Mozart, and Foster. Four hundred people came to the first Trapp Family Music Camp in 1944. Most had never played instruments or sang. Father Wasner taught the guests singing, starting with simple music. In ten days they sang beautifully. Daughter Maria gave recorder lessons. The sound of folk tunes was heard in the mountain air. Johanna cooked Austrian meals in the camp kitchen.

Singing, folk dancing, and art classes kept campers busy. They climbed Mount Mansfield for a picnic. Friendships were formed in the camp, and people returned each year. The camp continued for twelve singing summers.

"Please teach us to sing" is the letter P,
asked singers, who might be off-key.
And so the music camp got its start:
summertime friendships, songs, folk art.

P p

Rupert and Werner returned home safely when World War II ended in 1945. Two years later, in 1947, Captain von Trapp died. The gentle, fun-loving father was greatly missed. "He was a hero to us, all his life," said daughter Maria.

Rupert became a doctor, and was the first to marry. He left the singing group. Werner also married, but continued to sing. Johanna married and left home. Martina married a music camper, and sang until her death in 1951. In 1954 Eleonore married and left the group.

The Trapp Family Singers toured America every year. They revisited Austria on a European tour. They sang in Hawaii, South America, New Zealand, and Australia. Altogether they performed in thirty countries. "Music is an international language," Mother said. "It speaks from heart to heart."

But the time came for the Trapp Family Singers to stay home with their own children. Some were eager to explore new careers. In 1955 and 1956, the family made their farewell tour. For twenty years they had brought music to millions.

"Our lives are like a beautiful story," Mother said, "which just happened to be true."

Q is for Queens, kings, and presidents
who heard the family sing.
Music loved by millions—
Swedes, Australians, Italians, Brazilians.

The von Trapps discovered recorders in Austria and learned to play them. In America they introduced the flute-like instrument in their concerts and music camps.

The recorder was popular in medieval times. Composers like Bach, Georg Telemann, and Antonio Vivaldi used recorders in their works. The woodwind instrument comes in four sizes, which reflect its range of notes: soprano, alto, tenor, and bass.

Daughter Maria taught many musicians to enjoy playing recorder. She even wrote a recorder instruction book. Today the recorder is often called a child's instrument, since so many children learn to play it.

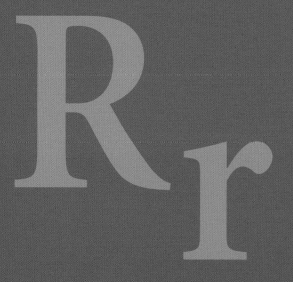

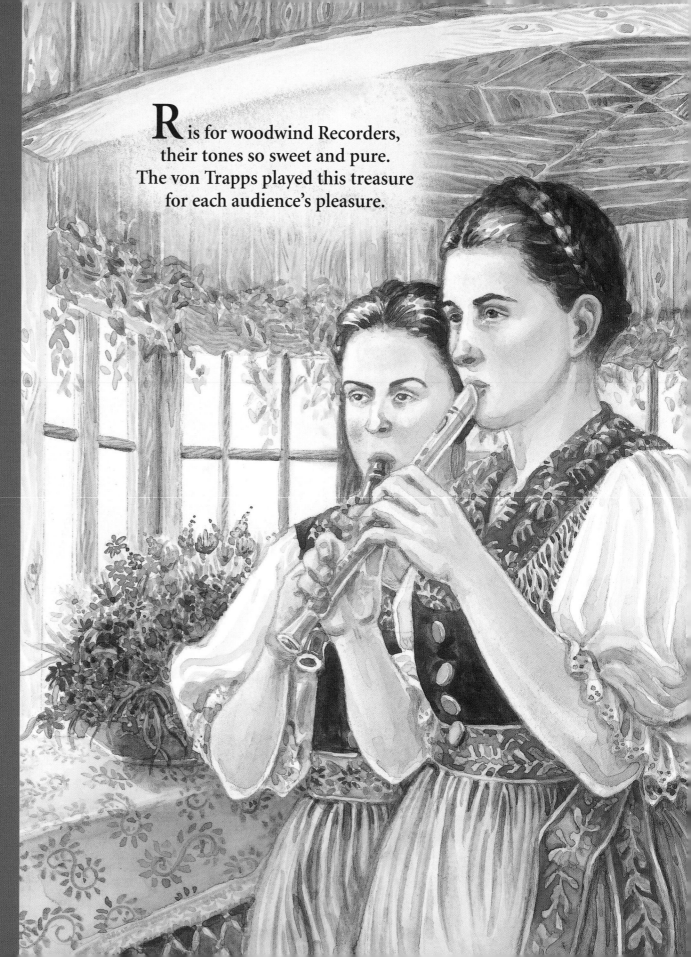

R is for woodwind Recorders,
their tones so sweet and pure.
The von Trapps played this treasure
for each audience's pleasure.

Two German movies were made in the 1950s about the von Trapp Family. These movies were popular around the world. In America the family's story became a musical play called *The Sound of Music*. It first appeared on the Broadway stage in New York City in 1959 and was very popular.

The play showed Maria's arrival as a teacher at the von Trapps', her marriage to the Captain, and the family's escape from Austria. Richard Rodgers and Oscar Hammerstein wrote songs for the play. Many are now familiar favorites: "Do-Re-Mi," "Climb Ev'ry Mountain," "My Favorite Things," and "Edelweiss."

In 1965 a movie version was released. Many scenes were filmed in Austria. Julie Andrews portrayed the role of Maria. The Captain was played by Christopher Plummer. The movie won almost every film award there is. Throughout the world, people have watched it in as many as 40 languages and dialects. *The Sound of Music* is the most successful movie musical ever made.

S is for *The Sound of Music,* a movie and a play
with songs we love
like "Do-Re-Mi."
A favorite story…forever it will be.

The von Trapps became forever famous because of *The Sound of Music.* When they saw the play and movie, they noticed that their names had been changed. They wished their beloved father had been portrayed as the kindly man he was. Both the play and movie made him far stricter than they remembered. *The Sound of Music* changed some of the family's history, but their faith, love, and patriotism were still part of the story.

"If you ask me how I like *The Sound of Music,*" said Maria von Trapp, "I will say, very much. But I was much wilder than Julie Andrews played me!"

When the family left home for concerts their rooms were rented to tourists. This was the beginning of the Trapp Family Lodge in Stowe, Vermont. When the singing tours ended, most of the children left home. Then the Lodge expanded to welcome more guests.

Mother Maria lived in the Lodge. She greeted guests, told stories, and answered questions about her life. "Are you homesick for Austria?" she was asked. "No," she answered. "I just look out at the Green Mountains and imagine the Austrian Alps, lying just behind."

Today the Lodge is much larger than the original family home, with 96 rooms. Guests hike and mountain bike through 2,400 acres of von Trapp land. In summer, music resounds from the Concert Meadow. The Lodge's Kids' Club is the place for children's fun.

It is exciting to meet a von Trapp at the Lodge. Family members give tours, telling of their past and present. "A little bit of Austria, a lot of Vermont" is the slogan at the Trapp Family Lodge.

T is for the Trapp Family Lodge
where you can hike and ski and bike.
Enjoy the mountain air
while meeting the von Trapps there!

Tt

Captain von Trapp's service to Austria as a U-boat commander was always remembered. He performed many heroic acts as captain of his submarine. His bravery in refusing to serve the Nazis became legend. After World War II he helped his homeland by founding the Trapp Family Austrian Relief. Americans gave food, clothing, and money for needy Austrians who were war victims. The Captain and his family collected the donations and sent them to Austria. Thousands were helped.

In 1997, fifty years after the Captain's death, Austria recognized his deeds. Cadets of Austria's military academy made the Captain their class hero. Daughter Maria visited the class, inviting them to come to the Trapp Family Lodge. Eighty-nine cadets traveled from Austria to Vermont to honor their hero.

Six of the Captain's living children gathered for the event at the Trapp Family Lodge. There were speeches, music, and a military salute to the Captain. Soldiers placed a wreath on the Captain's grave near the Lodge.

Captain von Trapp was always true to the motto of the Austrian soldiers: "Good Officers and Righteous Men."

U is for U-boat Captain Georg von Trapp,
forever an Austrian hero.
Years after the Captain's navy fame
Austria honored his famous name.

Even after their concert years, music remained important to the von Trapps. Their children grew up hearing them sing at reunions. When they sang, Werner's daughter Elisabeth listened. At eight, she studied piano and later played guitar. As a teenager Elisabeth sang and played guitar throughout Vermont. Elisabeth now performs in concerts around the world. She sings her own compositions, along with classical and folk music. She also performs songs from *The Sound of Music*. Elisabeth has portrayed her grandmother, Maria, in productions of the play.

"Music has given me a place to be," says Elisabeth. When she is not touring, she lives in the mountains of Vermont.

Elisabeth's nieces and nephews, The von Trapp Children, started singing for fun in their Montana home. Sofia, Melanie, Amanda, and Justin sang for church, for family, and for friends. When their grandfather Werner was sick, they recorded their singing for him.

Then came tours. The von Trapp Children travel the world, just as their ancestors did. Their concerts mix folk, gospel, classical music, and favorites from *The Sound of Music*. The children have also been actors in *The Sound of Music* productions.

The von Trapp Children are homeschooled, so they study while they travel. Traveling is great fun for them. At home they play sports, hike the Montana mountains near their home, and spend time with friends.

Vv

V is for von Trapp music
        still performed today.
Songs sung by family musicians
recalling *Sound of Music* traditions.

"So long, farewell, auf Wiedersehen, good-bye!" sang the von Trapp children in *The Sound of Music.* The real von Trapps also said many good-byes.

After their concert-touring days ended, Mother, Johannes, Maria, Rosmarie, and Father Wasner went to work as missionaries in New Guinea.

Martina died in childbirth in 1951. Hedwig taught school in Hawaii and Austria, where she died in 1972. Mother led a busy life at the Trapp Family Lodge and she died in 1987. Rupert, who worked as a doctor and raised six children, died in 1992. Johanna and her husband returned to Austria with their seven children. She died there in 1994. Werner farmed in Vermont with the help of some of his six children. He died in 2007.

Today, Agathe, who worked in a kindergarten, lives in Maryland. Maria lives near the Trapp Family Lodge. Rosmarie also lives near the Lodge. Eleonore and her husband live in Vermont. Their seven daughters and grandchildren visit often. Johannes has managed the Trapp Family Lodge for many years. His children now help him.

As Mother said, "There comes a time to say 'auf Wiedersehen,' but never to our memories and music."

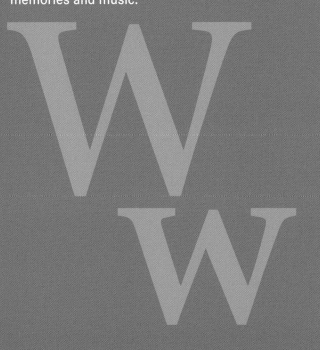

W is for *auf Wiedersehen*.
It means "Our visit now ends."
An Austrian saying, used by von Trapps
saying farewell to family and friends.

When Johannes was four, he started skiing with his family over the snowy Vermont hills. After long concert tours, he was happy to come back to the Green Mountains. He explored every trail around the Trapp Family Lodge. When Johannes was in college, friends joined him in cross-country skiing through the woods. He also introduced Lodge guests to his hobby.

"It was so much fun, I thought the public would like it," he said. "We simply had to share this beautiful place with people."

Johannes was trained as a forester and environmentalist. He carefully planned the ski trails, and extended them through the forest land at the Lodge.

The Trapp Family Lodge became America's first cross-country ski center. Now there are 28 groomed trails and 62 miles of back country trails. On winter days, hundreds of skiers wind through the woodland trails of the von Trapp land.

X is for Cross-country skiing,
gliding on a snow-covered trail.
Uphill you climb!
Downhill you'll sail!

Y is for Yodel, sung from peak to peak.
A mountain call, to share the news:
"Dinner's ready!" "Baby's born!"
Or "Just whose cow is whose?"

Yodeling originated in the Austrian mountains. Neighbors communicated with short yells, each with special meaning. Standing atop a mountain peak, the yodelers sound their call through the clear air. Yodeling is most effective when it echoes against rocks or mountains.

"The Echo Yodel" was a favorite in von Trapp concerts. Mother announced: "We bring our own echo from Vermont." The echo was Hedwig. She left the stage to provide the echo. When Martina made the first "call," Hedwig "echoed" in reply.

Children today learn "The Lonely Goatherd" from *The Sound of Music*. "La-de lay ee odl lay ee odl-oo" is a yodeling phrase from the song. It is fun to yodel, as Austrian mountain folk do.

Echoes of the original Trapp Family Singers are still heard. We can listen to their recordings, made long ago.

Yy

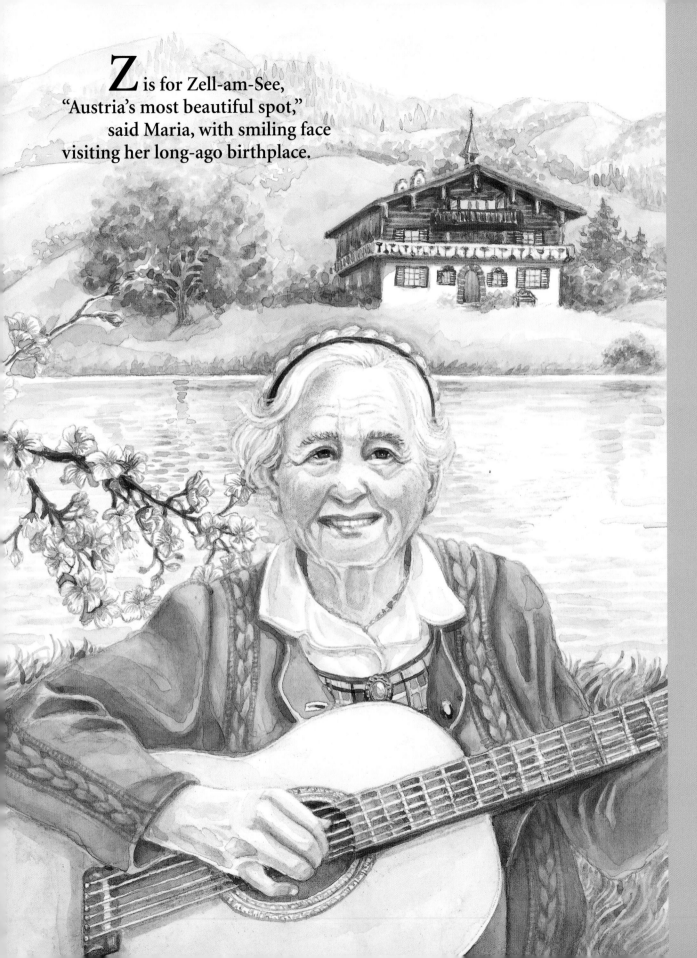

Z is for Zell-am-See,
"Austria's most beautiful spot,"
said Maria, with smiling face
visiting her long-ago birthplace.

In 2008 the von Trapps were back in Austria. Maria, her brother Johannes, and Werner's wife, Erika, were invited to Salzburg. Villa Trapp, the home the family left seventy years earlier, was now a hotel.

"I feel right at home," Maria said, as she walked though the door. In every room, there were memories of her father, her brothers and sisters, and her second mother. Here they had discovered the joy of singing! "There is power in music," Maria believes. "If the world sang together, there would be no war."

In Zell-am-See Maria visited her birthplace, the Erlhof. Nearby is her favorite mountain, the towering Kitzsteinhorn. "It is the pearl of Austria," Maria says.

In Austria, von Trapp is an honored name. And everywhere else around the world the members of the von Trapp family are legends—in song, story, and spirit.

Zz